Graduation Gift

Joseph Benric

Dedication

To my beautiful wife, thank you,
your love has lifted and carried me.
You inspire me to be a better person.
I Love You

To my amazing kids, anything
is possible. I hope this little
volume serves as a guide for
you. Love You, Dad.

Acknowledgments

To the countless people who have shared their knowledge and encouragement through their books, videos, websites and articles. Thank you. Special thanks to Steve Harvey, I heard you say, "If you can see it in your mind you can hold it in your hand" To Evan Carmichael, after each of your videos you ask, what action are you going to take? To Steve Maxwell, for the simple affirmation you use that helped me clear my mind. There are many, many more people I would like to acknowledge and thank, the best way I can think to do that is to ask all of you to continue putting out great content that touches all of our lives.

Hi I'm Joe,

I'm just getting started out in the world and I wanted to share a few things that could help you out. I hope it makes you chuckle a little and avoid some of life's pitfalls. In the back are some resource pages filled with links to websites, videos, articles and books that have served me well

and I hope they serve you too.

At Work...

Thinking about all the things
I want to have.

Reality...

Payday...

Time to buy some stuff...

Reality . . .

1st month $~~
Last month $~~
1 month Security $~~
The Landlord wants three months rent to sign the Lease.

A few days later...

End of the month...

First credit card bill...

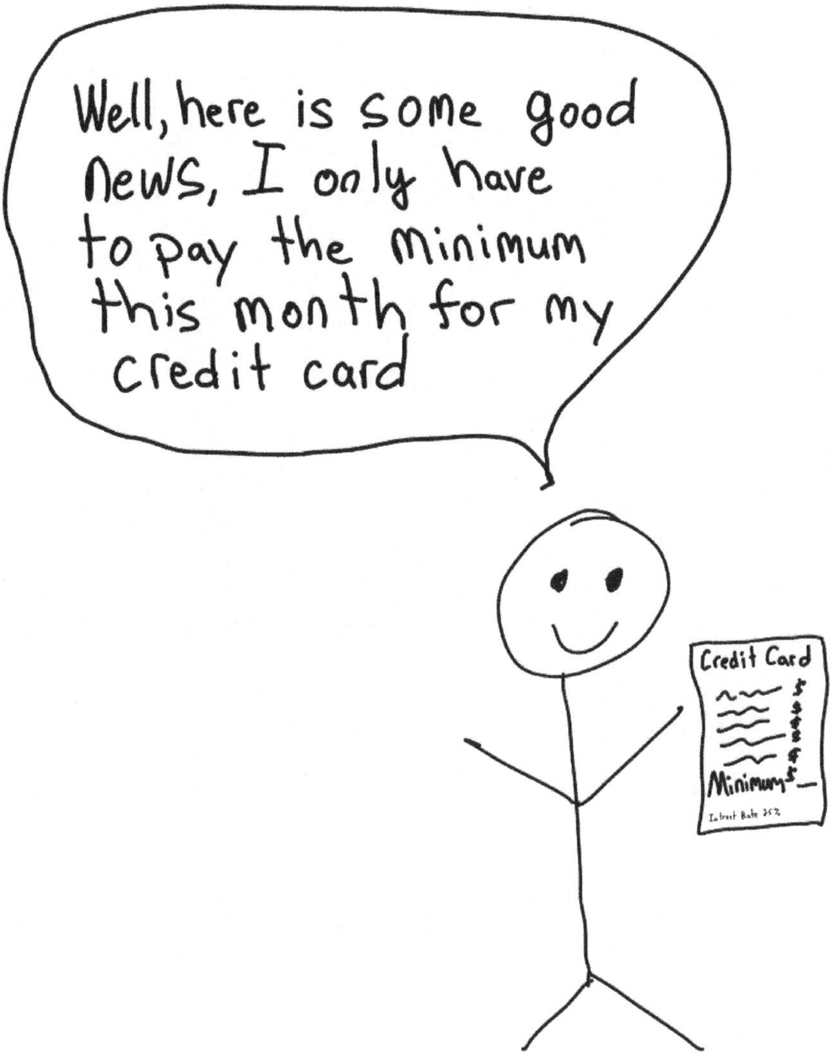

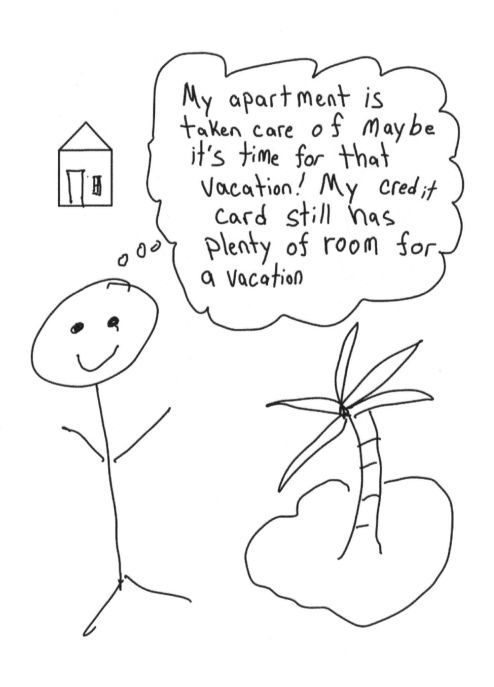

First day after vacation...

Two weeks later...

End of next month...

At a closer look . . .

If I pay only the Minimum, my $100 purchase will actually cost me about $300

I'm going to need a side hustle, What can I do right now with what I have?
I've got a lot of good ideas

A lot of these websites are saying I just have to get started and keep working at my ideas, no magic, just work. I can do that.

At a closer look...

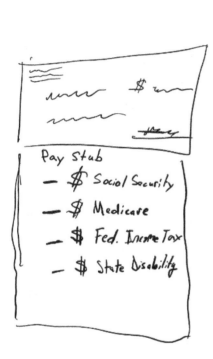

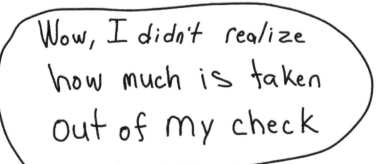

The goverment takes out almost 25% of what I make, then I have to pay sales tax on top of that when I buy stuff

A couple weeks later...

Not only can I act on my ideas but I should! If I Can see Something in my mind, I can do it.

A few days later...

At the store...

Store owner...

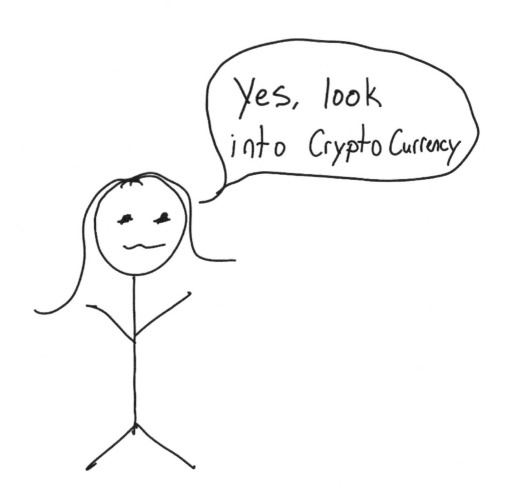

The lady at the store had some interesting things to say. I'm going to have to look that stuff up.

Visit to my Grandfather...

You gotta learn the language of money, a lot of times they use long fancy words that make it sound complicated

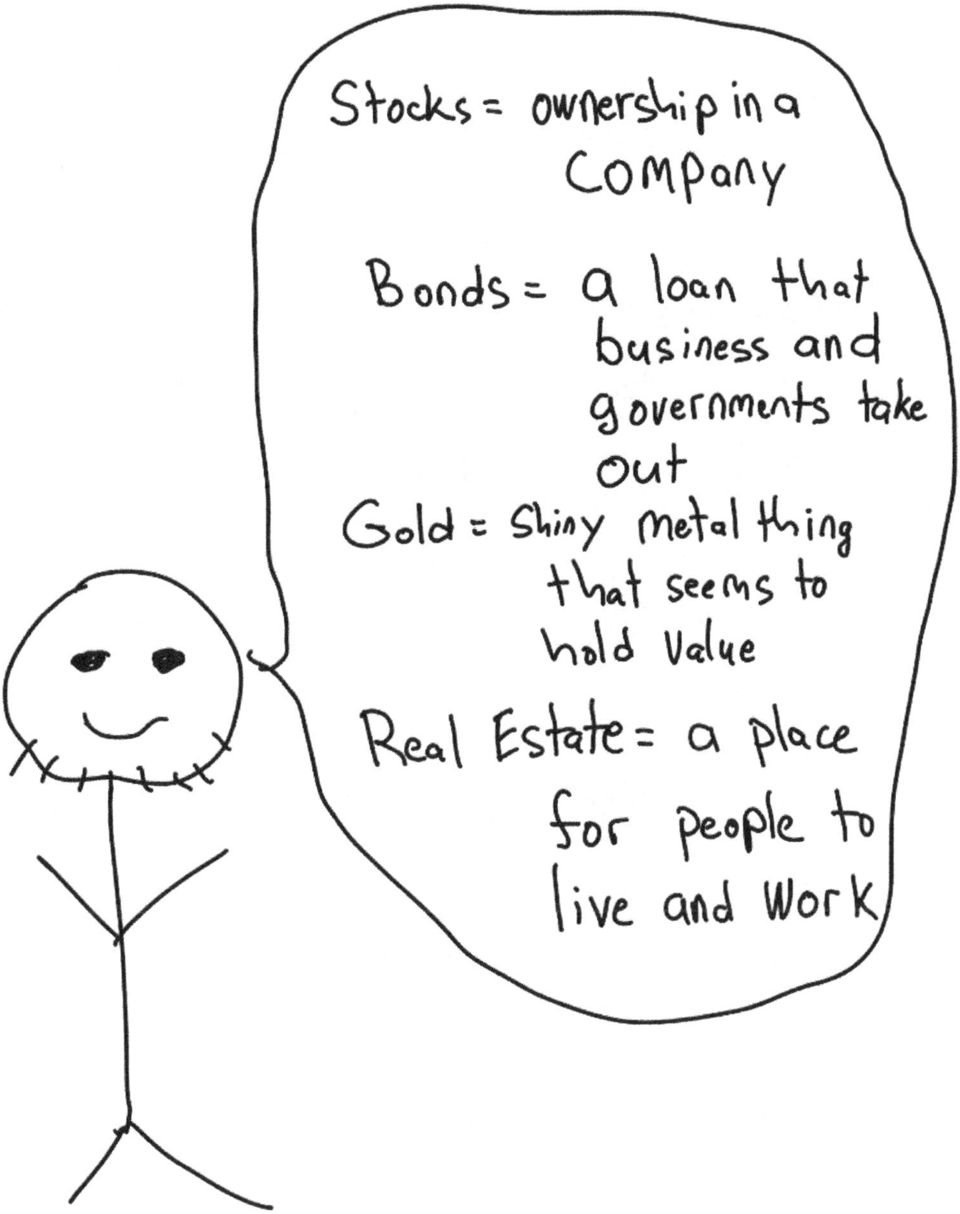
Stocks = ownership in a company
Bonds = a loan that business and governments take out
Gold = Shiny metal thing that seems to hold value
Real Estate = a place for people to live and work

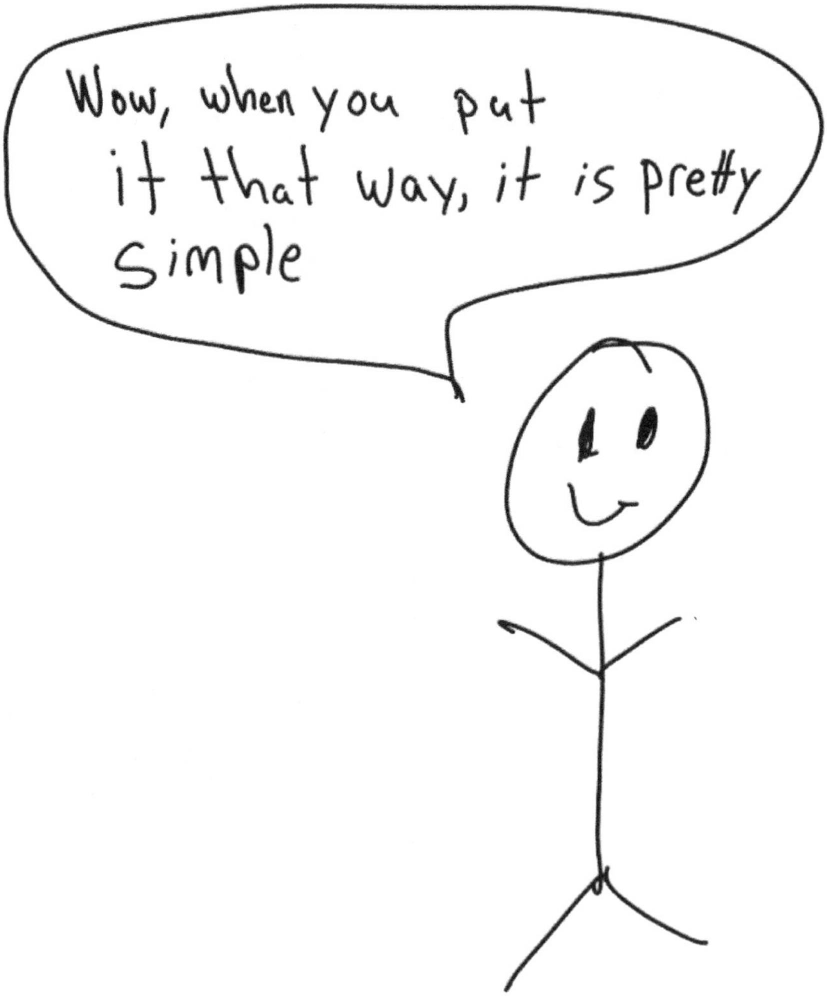
Wow, when you put it that way, it is pretty simple

Also,
Be happy and grateful for all the things you have going for you

Never forget the story about the man complaining that his shoes didn't fit so good until he walked in to a man in a wheelchair who had no legs.

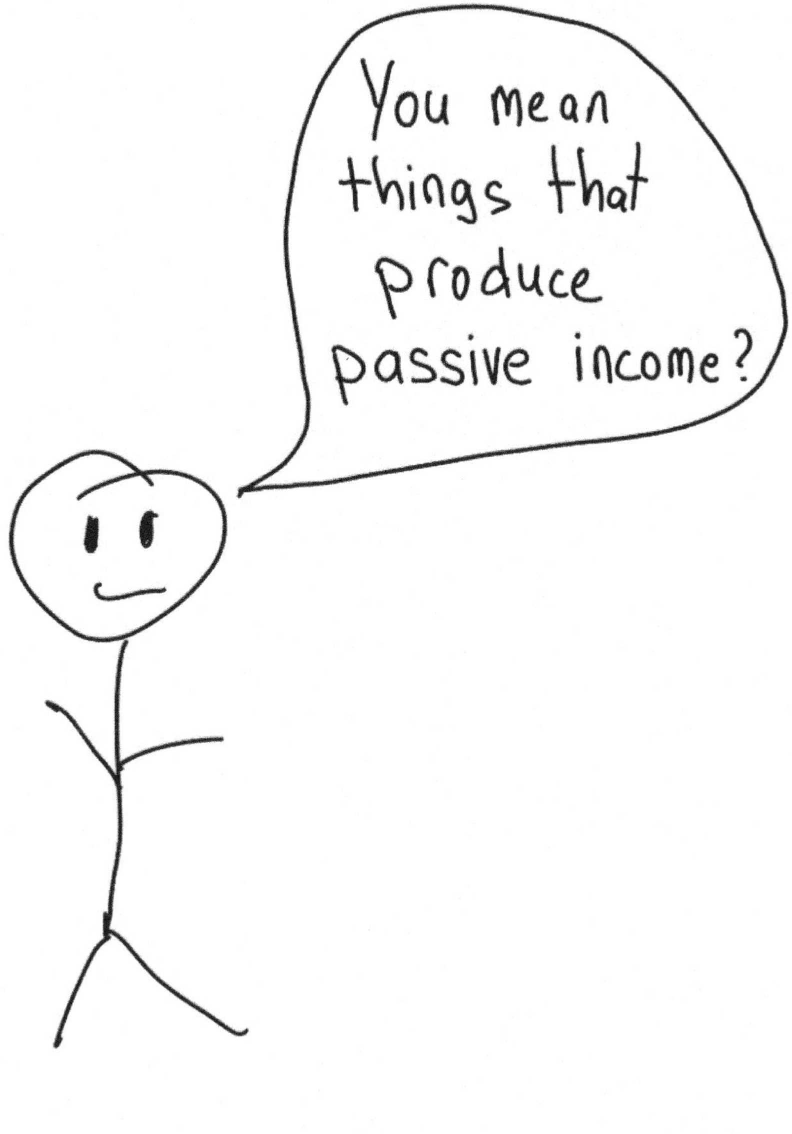
You mean things that produce passive income?

Yup, dividends, royalties, licensing fees, certain kinds of rent, things that pay you once you set it up whether you work or you don't work.

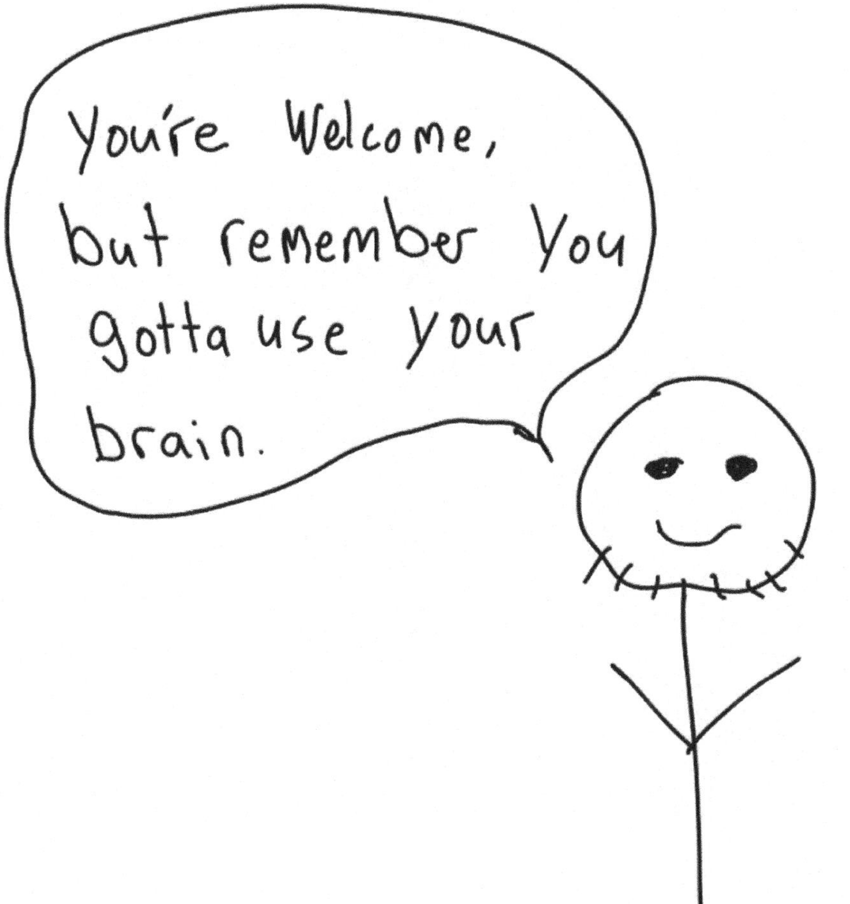
You're Welcome, but remember You gotta use your brain.

Back at home ...

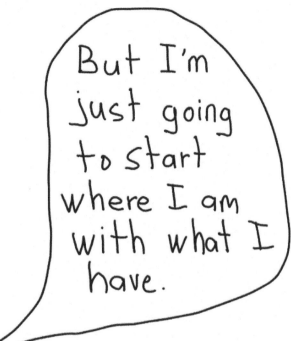

Why I wrote this book.

I went through four years of high school and four years of college and did not receive any personal management classes or lessons. Then I watched my kids go through school and they did not get any information about this subject. So, I thought, after much griping about how personal finance and management are not being taught, that I should write about it. I tried to cover so many different topics from imagination, to finance, attitude, goals, the willingness to try and asking for help. So many things that are not covered in school that would be useful in your day-to-day life. I wrote this book with little or no editing using my own handwriting. I did this intentionally, I wanted to show that you don't have to be neat or smart, you don't have to be the best, you don't have to wait till it's perfect, you just have to start and do it. You must act, when you have an idea, you have to get in motion and act on your idea. **Write down things you want**, whatever is in your head just write it down. Then figure out what you have to do to get what you want. Don't announce your thoughts and ideas to the world yet, get into action and start working on it. Figure out the things you need to do, the people who can help and the things you need to learn and get on with it. If it's legal, honest and moral there is nothing you cannot do, there is nothing you cannot have, there is nothing you cannot be.

How I wrote this book.

I wrote this book on an iPad with an app called Notability. I wrote a rough draft that was mostly notes and strange drawings that looked like chicken scratch. Then I rewrote it at a slower pace in my handwriting which I think most people can read. The actual writing and illustrating took about five weeks, the ideas and notes for the book are the product over 8 years of me thinking I am going to write a book until one day I just decided to write it, then it only took six weeks in total. Once I had a clean copy, I transferred the images from Notability to my desktop by email. Then I downloaded a template from Kindle Direct Publishing (KDP) I chose the 7.5 x 9.25 format. I entered my images into Word page by page, this took a couple of days, keep in mind that I have no writing or publishing experience and had to learn from the school of Google and YouTube as I went along. KDP also has a great tutorial on their website on how to write and publish on their platform. Along the way I got an ISBN number (International Standard Book Number) from bowker.com, once I had my book formatted properly on Word, I saved it as a PDF then downloaded it to the KDP website. From there it goes to the KDP editor, if it is approved it can go to publication. I chose to have a few copies printed and sent to me before I released it to the public to make sure the printed version looked and felt the way I intended. I also had my final version of the book copyrighted. At this point I made a few clicks on the KDP platform and my book went live to the public. I just wrote and published my first book.

Resource Pages

This is not financial advice or life advice; these are things that have helped me, and I wanted to share them with you.

Imagination

Steve Harvey, Imagination is everything, presented by The Official Steve Harvey (June 10, 2019)
https://youtu.be/TbEMIw3ecGI

Wayne Dyer, This Really Works! It Really Does Work, presented by Video Advice (January 19, 2020)
https://youtu.be/BWEy8brAuRA

One of the Most Motivational Videos You'll Ever See [WARNING!!! – Belief Changer], presented by Video Advice (September 25, 2017)
https://youtu.be/znwRzsYLr6s

The Magic of Thinking Big, David J. Schwartz, PH. D.
Available on Amazon

Job Related

www.thebalancecareers.com

How to Find a Job in 2021 – Fast, presented by Professor Nez (December 17, 2020)
https://www.youtube.com/watch?v=VoUSp-a23Ys

How To Write The Perfect Resume, by Dan Clay
Available on Amazon

How to Write a Killer LinkedIn Profile, by Brenda Bernstein
Available on Amazon

Job Search
www.Indeed.com

Your Paycheck

Paycheck: What Is It? by Susan M. Heathfield (September 28, 2020)
https://www.thebalancecareers.com/what-is-a-paycheck-1918222

When You Can Expect to Get Your First and Last Paycheck, by Alison
Doyle (April 20, 2021)
https://www.thebalancecareers.com/when-you-can-expect-to-get-
your-first-and-lastpaycheck-2060057
www.thebalancecareers.com

Your First Paycheck: Explained, by Sarah Walker Caron presented by
themuse.com
https://www.themuse.com/advice/your-first-paycheck-explained

6 Important Things You Need to Know About Your Paycheck,
presented by CheckMark.com
https://blog.checkmark.com/understanding-your-paycheck/
www.checkmark.com

First Credit Card

First-Time Cardholder? Avoid These 5 Common Credit Card Mistakes,
by Dan Rafter (July 5, 2018)

https://www.creditcards.com/credit-card-news/first-credit-card-mistakes/

Benefits of your Credit Card, presented by Mission Lane
https://youtu.be/w_DSNPDrD5M

How do Credit Cards Work? A Beginner's Guide, by Kevin Joey Chen (August 10, 2020) presented by Finder.com
https://www.finder.com/credit-cards-101

Debt Management and Credit Cards, presented by www.howstuffworks.com
https://money.howstuffworks.com/personal-finance/debt-management/credit-card2.htm

Credit Card Interest Calculator
https://www.cardratings.com/credit-card-interest-calculator.html

Savings Accounts

What is a Savings Account by Rebecca Lake and Daphne Forman (February 21, 2021)
https://www.forbes.com/advisor/banking/how-savings-accounts-work/

How Does Savings Account Interest Work? Discover Bank (October 10, 20217)
https://www.youtube.com/watch?v=8edPzh71RIQ

How do Savings Accounts Work? presented by Howstuffworks.com
https://money.howstuffworks.com/personal-finance/budgeting/savings-accounts.htm

Renting a Home

How to Get Your First Apartment, by Miriam Caldwell (October 24, 2020) presented by thebalance.com
https://www.thebalance.com/how-to-rent-your-first-apartment-2385952

The Ultimate First Apartment Guide and Check List, presented by Bellhop
https://www.getbellhops.com/blog/the-ultimate-first-apartment-guide-and-checklist/
www.getbellhops.com

How to Rent Your First Apartment: Apartment Guide and Checklist, by Sania Tran (October 24, 2018)
https://www.apartmentlist.com/renter-life/first-time-renter-apartment-guide-checklist

How Apartment Leases Work, by Brian Boone (updated February 11, 2021)
https://home.howstuffworks.com/real-estate/apartment-lease.htm

Sample Lease, Blumberg Lease for New York Residential
https://www.blumberg.com/invoice.cgi?rm=view_cluster;cluster_id=1762952#preview-1
www.Blumberg.com

What Things Really Cost

9 Things That Cost You Surprisingly More Than You Think, by Jeffrey Trull
https://ptmoney.com/the-surprising-true-costs-of-9-common-expenses/

What Things Really Cost, presented by spreadsheetshoppe.com
https://www.spreadsheetshoppe.com/what-things-really-cost/

How Well Do You Know How Much These Common Items Cost In the US?, by Gabrielle Olya (March 11, 2021)
https://www.gobankingrates.com/money/economy/how-much-common-items-cost-us/

Fulfillment

Joe Rogan's Speech No One Wants to HEAR and ADMIT, presented by Motivation Core (April 5, 2021)
https://www.youtube.com/watch?v=CKoi3biNt-c

Steve Job's Speech Will Leave You SPEECHLESS, presented by Business Core (April 20, 2021)
https://www.youtube.com/watch?v=-Pd-LBZ2lHw

How to Spend Your Money

Larry Alton, Here's How You Should Really Be Spending Your Paycheck presented by inc.com
https://www.inc.com/larry-alton/heres-how-you-should-really-be-spending-your-paycheck.html

The Cost of Credit Cards

The Real Cost Of Credit Card Interest Rates
https://credit.org/blog/real-cost-credit-card-interest-rates/

Jason with Honest Finance, Paying the Minimum on Your Credit Cards! (What Happens?) June 23, 2020
https://www.youtube.com/watch?v=Y7xfcMhchT0

Credit Card Interest Calculator, presented by cardratings.com
https://www.cardratings.com/credit-card-interest-calculator.html

A Better Way

A Quick and Really Fun Overview of the Go-Giver, presented by Bob Burg (March 8, 2013)
https://www.youtube.com/watch?v=TNjNuFjn4hM

The Go Giver by Bob Burg and John David Mann
Available on Amazon

How to Be Happy- Best Motivational Speech, presented by Motivational Videos (Nov 18, 2020)
https://www.youtube.com/watch?v=oWIqWaMqBTM&list=LL&index=8

Joe Rogan, Speech Will Leave you Speachless -One of the Most Eye Opening Motivational Videos Ever, presented by Motivation Core
https://www.youtube.com/watch?v=LFX_tyicBT4&t=0s

Learning from DIRTY JOBS – Mike Rowe's Best ADVICE – Top 10 Rules, presented by Evan Charmichael (Oct 23, 2019)
https://www.youtube.com/watch?v=zWFW4EJoGyk

Self Help

Even Carmichael, Be Prepared to Do Difficult Things! Evan Carmichael - Top 10 Rules, presented by Evan Carmichael (May 8, 2020)
https://www.youtube.com/watch?v=fK7ggnTwmWk&list=LL&index=39
https://believe.evancarmichael.com/homepage

John Assaraf, Train Your Brain to Make More Money, presented by Team Fearless (January 29, 2018)
https://www.youtube.com/watch?v=BrRZZ_8NTkg&list=LL&index=41

John Assaraf, Are You Interested or Are You Committed? presented by Team Fearless (January 1, 2018)
https://www.youtube.com/watch?v=NrloYLC-KtM&list=LL&index=27

David Goggins, Master Your Mind – Motivational Video Ft. David Goggins (Prison of The Mind), presented by Team Fearless Oct 7, 2019
https://www.youtube.com/watch?v=sJmiQosST94&list=WL&index=59

Attitude

Steve Maxwell on London Real, Mind Control – The Power of Positive Thinking, presented by London Real (Sept 7, 2015)
https://www.youtube.com/watch?v=XmmXP7IGsNA

Denzel Washington, WATCH THIS EVERYDAY AND CHANGE YOUR LIFE -Denzel Washington Motivational Speech 2020, presented by AlexKaltsMotivation (June 3, 2019)
https://www.youtube.com/watch?v=tbnzAVRZ9Xc&list=LL&index=69

David Goggins, The Most Motivating 6 Minutes of Your Life – David Goggins, presented by Video Advice (January 16, 2019)
https://www.youtube.com/watch?v=Zy5c2k3W458&list=LL&index=68

Robert Greene on Impact Theory, Why Attitude is Everything, presented by Succes Chasers (January 1, 2019)
https://www.youtube.com/watch?v=KxADX7UuG2E

It Will Give You Goosebumps – Elon Musk Tribute, presented by Business Core (March 4, 2021)
https://www.youtube.com/watch?v=MIBlwo1nQ9s

Wealth

A Quick and Really Fun Overview of the Go-Giver, presented by Bob Burg (March 8, 2013)
https://www.youtube.com/watch?v=TNjNuFjn4hM

The Go Giver, by Bob Burg and John David Man
Available on Amazon

How to Be Happy- Best Motivational Speech, presented by Motivational Videos (November 18, 2020)
https://www.youtube.com/watch?v=oWIqWaMqBTM&list=LL&index=8

Earl Nightingale, Change Your Life in 19 Minutes, presented by Andrea Callahan International, Inc. (October 20, 2014)
https://www.youtube.com/watch?v=6tbHYvH347A&list=WL&index=33

Napoleon Hill's, Think and Grow Rich Book Summary by 2000 Books presented by Evan Carmichael (December 7, 2018)
https://www.youtube.com/watch?v=sm9pNiYpiDY&list=LL&index=53

Napoleon Hill, Think and Grow Rich
Available On Amazon

John Frederick Demartini, The Most Honest Advice About Getting Rich, presented by Video Advice (September 25, 2019)
https://www.youtube.com/watch?v=cbjyMfwRCPA

Write it Down

Joe Rogan, , That's Why Joe Rogan is a Genius of Motivation presented by Motivation Core (October 31, 2020)
https://www.youtube.com/watch?v=EFqIQh48ico&list=LL&index=11

Steve Harvey, Write Your Vision, presented by The Official Steve Harvey (September 15, 2019) steveharvey.com
https://www.youtube.com/watch?v=DlMAIYd7-J4

Bob Proctor (@bobproctorLIVE), Get a BIG Idea, Get Motivated and Take Action!, presented by Evan Carmichael (December 26, 2018)
https://www.youtube.com/watch?v=8LjFHyllZtI

Getting Started

Steve Harvey, Start Today, presented by Above Inspiration (March 1, 2018)
https://www.youtube.com/watch?v=RNWNVl955g4

Peter McKinnon, Just START Right NOW!, presented by Evan Carmichael (April 24, 2018)
https://www.youtube.com/watch?v=jcla4oUQY44

Marie Forleo, Can't Get Started? This One Idea Could Change Your Life presented by Marie Forleo (March 7, 2017)
https://www.youtube.com/watch?v=TmZf61ZkcSY&list=LL&index=6

Where Am I spending My Money?

Shay Budgets, How To: The Easiest and Simplest Way To Create a Monthly Budget 6-Minutes Process, presented by Shay Budgets (July 19, 2019)
https://www.youtube.com/watch?v=3pslPbfpnzk

Cap & Compass, Life After School. Explained. The Definitive Reference Guide
Available on Amazon

Paxton/Patterson, Understanding Your Paycheck, presented by Paxton/Patterson (May 19, 2017)
https://www.youtube.com/watch?v=XQof87stf_o

Taxes

How Taxes Affect Your Paycheck, presented by IGrad Inc. (March 17, 2021)
https://www.igrad.com/infographics/how-taxes-affect-your-paycheck

How Do Tax Brackets Actually Work? , presented by Two Cents (August 21, 2019)
https://www.youtube.com/watch?v=6cRg9bnSnvg

Do We Actually Need Taxes? Presented by Economics Explained (June 4, 2020)
https://www.youtube.com/watch?v=xfmUrw0gDiU

Tom Wheelwright, CPA, Tax-Free Wealth: How to Build Massive Wealth by Permanently Lowering Your Taxes (Rich Dad's Advisors) June 26, 2018
Available on Amazon

A Ten Dollar Idea

Steve Harvey Tells You How To Make A Million Dollars, presented by The Official Steve Harvey (April 27, 2015)
https://www.youtube.com/watch?v=vC_44E2N4OY

Inflation

Fractional Reserve Banking (The Banking System Explained), presented by Chris Invests (June 28, 2020)
https://www.youtube.com/watch?v=vVZ48_V_dKQ

Ben Felix, Understanding the Fed's "Money Printer" (QE, the Stock Market, and Inflation), presented by Ben Felix (Jul 31, 2020)
https://www.youtube.com/watch?v=K3lP3BhvnSo

Understanding Inflation, presented by WyattStorch.com
https://wyattstorch.info/2019/10/understanding-inflation-2/

What They Don't Teach Us in School

Stephen Guise stephenguise.com , How School Trains Us To Fail In the Real World, presented by Explorist (Oct 28, 2018)
https://www.youtube.com/watch?v=ryxh-Pd9dJU

Quit My $100K Job After Realizing This (WHAT NOBODY TAUGHT YOU ABOUT MONEY), presented by Investing with Rose (Jul 8, 2020)
https://www.youtube.com/watch?v=N1exmvOx-2A

Patrick Bet-David, 15 Things School Won't Teach You, presented by Valuetainment (Jan 12, 2021)
https://www.youtube.com/watch?v=zAAfmUGDeCk

Back to School (1986) Movie clip – Thornton Talks Business Scene provided by Movieclips
https://www.youtube.com/watch?v=uSLscJ2cYo4&list=WL&index=58

They Want You To Be Poor, An Eye Opening Interview, presented by Be Inspired (March 5, 2019)
https://www.youtube.com/watch?v=m6pWEzkbnDE

Robert Kiyosaki – Rich Dad, Poor Dad – How to Invest In Yourself – Part 1/2 , presented by London Real (Feb 24,2019)
https://www.youtube.com/watch?v=d5FVFsG8NmI&t=333s

Crypto Currency

DAN Teaches Crypto – Helping People Understand What is...
www.danteachescrypto.com

Digital Asset News, Bite Sized Crypto News
https://www.youtube.com/channel/UCJgHxpqfhWEEjYH9cLXqhIQ

How Does a Blockchain Work? presented by www.bitpanda.com
https://www.bitpanda.com/academy/en/lessons/how-does-a-blockchain-work/

You Have to Ask

Steve Harvey Uncut: You Have Not Because You Ask Not! Presented by Steve TV Show (December 31, 2015)
https://www.youtube.com/watch?v=dtprAPix2a0

The Language of Money

Jessica Martel, Definitions That Will Make You Sound Like An Investing Pro (December 23, 2020)
https://www.moneyunder30.com/investing-terms-and-definitions

The Go Giver, by Bob Burg and John David Man, Gildan Media LLC 2015
Available on Amazon

Rich Dad Poor Dad Summary (Animated), presented by Chronicle Living (June 5, 2017)
https://www.youtube.com/watch?v=TcNpoc-lF0M

Robert T. Kiyosaki, Rich Dad Poor Dad: What the Rich Teach Their Kids About Money That the Poor and Middle Class Do Not! Mass Market Paperback (April 11, 2017)
Available on Amazon

Gratitude

You Need To Do This In The Morning! It Will Change Your Entire Day!, presented by Be Inspired (July 4, 2018)
https://www.youtube.com/watch?v=ni_HDRKPnJk&list=LL&index=43

Morgan Freeman and Wayne Dyer, You Are The Creator – Warning: This might shake up your belief system, presented by Video Advice (February 9, 2018)
https://www.youtube.com/watch?v=r7cYsgB4G1s

Passive Income

The Passive Income Playbook: The Simple, Proven, Step-by-Step System You Can Use in the Next 30 Days, by Raza Imam
Available on Amazon

9 Passive Income Ideas – How I Make $27k Week, presented by Ali Abdaal (April 15, 2021)
https://www.youtube.com/watch?v=M5y69v1RbU0&list=LL&index=11

Self-Publishing

Sarah Cordiner, How to PUBLISH a Children's Book on AMAZON in 10 Minutes! (December 30, 2019)
https://www.moneyunder30.com/investing-terms-and-definitions

Stefan James, How To Self-Publish A Book On Amazon (Step-By-Step Tutorial), presented by Project Life Mastery (August 20, 2020)
https://www.youtube.com/watch?v=gRY3d5aBiUI&list=WL&index=4